J 709.04 [handwritten]

W9-BSC-707

DISCARD

20.95

ART PROFILES
For Kids

EDVARD MUNCH

Mitchell Lane
PUBLISHERS

P.O. Box 196
Hockessin, Delaware 19707
Visit us on the web: www.mitchelllane.com
Comments? email us: mitchelllane@mitchelllane.com

ART PROFILES FOR KIDS

Titles in the Series

Art Profiles
For Kids
EDVARD MUNCH

Jim Whiting

Mitchell Lane
PUBLISHERS

P.O. Box 196
Hockessin, Delaware 19707
Visit us on the web: www.mitchelllane.com
Comments? email us: mitchelllane@mitchelllane.com

Printing   1   2   3   4   5   6   7   8   9

Library of Congress Cataloging-in-Publication Data
Whiting, Jim, 1943–
Edvard Munch / by Jim Whiting.
    p. cm.—(Art profiles for kids)
Includes bibliographical references and index.
ISBN 978-1-58415-712-0 (library bound)
1. Munch, Edvard, 1863–1944—Juvenile literature. 2. Artists—Norway—Biography—Juvenile literature. 1. Munch, Edvard, 1863–1944. II. Title.
N7073.M8W46 2009
760.092—dc22
[B]
                                                                    2008002250

ABOUT THE AUTHOR: Jim Whiting has been a remarkably versatile and accomplished journalist, writer, editor, and photographer for more than 30 years. He has long been fascinated by the works of Vincent van Gogh and has seen many firsthand. An avid reader since early childhood, Mr. Whiting has written and edited over 200 nonfiction children's books, including *William Shakespeare, Hercules,* and *Michelangelo* for Mitchell Lane Publishers. He lives in Washington State with his wife.

ABOUT THE COVER: The images on the cover are paintings by the various artists in this series.

PHOTO CREDITS: p. 13—painted by Rembrandt; p. 41—sculpted by Gustav Vigeland; all other paintings are credited to Edvard Munch

PUBLISHER'S NOTE: The facts on which this story is based have been thoroughly researched. Documentation of such research appears on page 46. While every possible effort has been made to ensure accuracy, the publisher will not assume liability for damages caused by inaccuracies in the data, and makes no warranty on the accuracy of the information contained herein.

PLB

Norwegian painter Edvard Munch's *The Scream* is one of the world's most recognizable paintings. Though it was painted in 1893, it was based on an experience Munch had nearly a decade earlier. He was walking at sunset with two friends. Suddenly he heard a scream—but it was just inside his head. His friends had no idea what was happening and kept walking.

one

Stolen—and Stolen Again!

In the predawn darkness on February 12, 1994, nervous athletes began awakening in the town of Lillehammer, Norway. That evening, thousands of them would march into the Lysgardsbakken Ski Jumping Arena for the opening ceremonies of the Winter Olympics. Countless numbers of television viewers would watch their entrance. The Norwegians were eager to showcase their country to the world.

About 100 miles to the south in Oslo, Norway's capital, two men were about to make their own appearance on television. No one—including the one person who was being paid to watch—would see their entrance until it was too late.

The two men were parked next to the National Gallery, the city's leading art museum. They ran across the snow to some bushes at the front of the museum, pulled out a ladder they had hidden there, and leaned it against the building. One man began climbing. He nearly made it to the top before losing his grip and falling. He brushed himself off and went up again. When he reached the top, he smashed a window with a hammer.

A television camera caught his performance. So did the museum's alarm system, which blared when the glass was broken. The one guard on duty was in the basement. He had been working at the museum for less than two months and thought the alarm was false. His shift was nearly over and he still had paperwork to fill out. The harsh noise interrupted his concentration, so he hurried over to the control panel, flipped the alarm off, and returned to his desk. He didn't bother looking at the TV monitors.

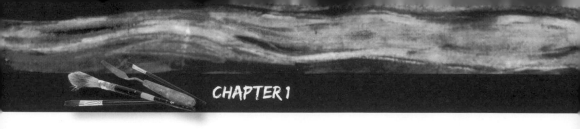

The man who had broken the window bounded through the opening in the shattered glass and into the museum's main gallery. It featured an exhibition by Norway's most famous painter, Edvard Munch (pronounced MOOHNK). Fifty-six of the artist's works were on display, but the intruder was interested in only one: *The Scream.*

The Scream was by far Munch's most famous painting, on the same level as Leonardo da Vinci's *Mona Lisa* or Vincent van Gogh's *Starry Night* in terms of popularity and recognizability. In addition to countless numbers of prints, the famous work had appeared on advertisements, coffee mugs, T-shirts, and Halloween masks; a parody of it was even featured on an episode of the cartoon *The Simpsons.* The painting was valued at $72 million.

Organizers of the exhibit had made the two thieves' task considerably easier. They moved the exhibit down one floor to make access easier for visitors. They hung *The Scream* next to a window. There were no protective bars on the windows, which were made of ordinary, rather than reinforced, glass. They used a single wire to suspend the painting instead of securely bolting it to the wall.

The intruder snipped the wire and the painting fell into his arms. He slid it down the ladder to his accomplice, then quickly climbed back to the ground. The two men ran to their car, tossed the painting inside, and roared away. The robbery had taken less than three minutes.

The two men had timed their exploit to coincide with the opening of the Olympics. Norway, which had expected to bask in the glory of the Games, now faced not only worldwide ridicule but also embarrassment at the ease with which its most famous work of art had vanished.

"In this beautiful scenery, it is hard to imagine that such evil things could take place,"[1] complained the country's minister of culture.

There was another concern. *The Scream* was painted on cardboard, rather than canvas, and a few portions had been chalked in. It was extremely fragile.

The police had no leads. In desperation, the National Gallery turned to Charley Hill, a British detective who had been very successful in retrieving stolen art.

Hill was all too aware that art theft is highly profitable. With many other crimes to investigate, police can devote just a limited amount of time and effort to stolen art. Only about three percent of art thieves are captured; less than ten percent of the irreplaceable works are recovered.

Unlike banks, which keep their money carefully guarded in secure vaults, art museums have to keep their treasures out in public view. In addition, many museums are seriously underfunded and reluctant to commit much money to security. One American security company reportedly paid its employees fifty cents less per hour than McDonald's. As a result, according to security specialist Steven Keller, "The people protecting our art are the ones who couldn't get jobs flipping burgers."[2]

The thieves, who had posed as museum visitors on several occasions, were aware of the gallery's shortcomings. They scribbled, "Thanks for the poor security"[3] on a postcard they left behind.

With little to go on, Hill undertook the assignment of recovering *The Scream*. In normal police work, apprehending felons is the primary goal, but that isn't necessarily the case with art theft. As author Edward Dolnick explains, "Kicking down a door and shouting 'Police!' was all very well, but where was the painting?"[4]

The Scream was far too famous to be sold openly, so Hill believed the thieves would hold it for ransom. Since the Norwegian parliament would never pay public money to get the painting back, that left private money as the only option—and the best source of private money was more than 5,000 miles away.

That was the Getty Museum in Los Angeles. It had been established by oil billionaire J. Paul Getty, at one point the world's richest man. He left the bulk of his fortune to the museum, which opened in 1997. Charley Hill decided to go undercover by posing as Christopher Roberts, a representative of the Getty Museum, and get the word out that he was willing to pay big bucks for *The Scream*.

The plan was risky. Hill was British, but he had to be able to speak like an American. If he made contact with the thieves and they broke his cover, they might kill him.

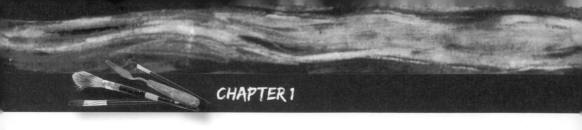
About two and a half months after the theft, a newspaper reporter followed a tip and found a piece of the frame. Soon afterward, the thieves contacted a Norwegian art dealer. In turn, the art dealer contacted "Roberts" and suggested that he come to Oslo—with cash. About half a million dollars in cash.

Hill arrived in Oslo around noon on May 5 and met with the art dealer and a man who, it seemed certain, was one of the thieves. Events moved rapidly after that. Just over forty-eight hours later, Hill held what he was told was *The Scream*. It was covered with a blue bedsheet. He removed the covering, only to see a crude charcoal drawing that vaguely resembled the famous painting. For a moment, he was afraid that the crooks had misled him. Then he turned it over.

It was *The Scream*.

"Hill held the painting up and scanned it, savoring the kind of opportunity that he knew only came along a few times in a lifetime," notes Dolnick. "No frame, no glass, no hovering guards, no crowds, nothing between you and a few square feet of sublime achievement."[5]

Two men were arrested for their involvement, and two more were taken into custody soon afterward. One was Pål Enger, a former soccer player for one of Norway's top professional teams. He had developed a taste for publicity and cultivated it when he turned his talents to crime. "I was not one of the best [at soccer] but I was one of the best in the criminal world, and I thought it would be more fun to play on the team where I was best,"[6] he boasted.

Enger already had a history of stealing Munch paintings. Six years earlier, he had stolen Munch's *The Vampire*. Though he denied being involved with the *Scream* theft, because of his reputation, he posed for pictures in the space where the painting had hung. While it clearly wasn't an admission of guilt, he inserted an announcement in a local paper when his wife gave birth two months after the theft: The baby had come into the world "with a Scream!"[7] When police scanned security video taken five days before the theft, Enger was clearly visible.

He and three other men were convicted of the crime and sentenced to prison. A Norwegian appeals court freed all but Enger, who stoutly maintained

Painted in 1893–1894, Munch's *The Vampire* shows a woman with her teeth in a man's neck. Her red hair falls over his head and helps maintain her grip on him. Many of Munch's paintings reflect this theme, that love between a man and woman can be destructive.

his innocence but almost certainly was one of the two men who had broken into the National Gallery. The court ruled that Hill's testimony couldn't be used because he had come into the country under a false name.

Just over a decade later, newspaper headlines again announced, "The Scream Is Stolen." It wasn't the same painting: Munch, as was his habit, had actually made several versions. This new theft involved one in the Munch Museum in Oslo.

There were no early-morning escapades this time. Two men brandishing guns stormed their way into the gallery at midday. Terrified patrons could only watch as one man grabbed *The Scream* and his accomplice took down *Madonna*, another Munch masterpiece. They ran outside, hurled the paintings into a car driven by a third man, and sped off. The rough handling alarmed museum officials, who were afraid the paintings would be damaged.

Their fears were justified. Unlike the men who stole the other *Scream*, these thieves had no interest in making money from their crime. Rather, they were trying to draw attention away from a notorious armed robbery that had taken place several months earlier. Because a detective had been shot to death—highly unusual in Norway, which has one of the world's lowest rates of gun violence—virtually all of the slain man's colleagues were working the case. Taking *The Scream* was an effort to divert attention and resources from the investigation.

The effort didn't succeed. In the spring of 2006, three men were arrested, but there was no sign of either painting.

Finally, in August of that year, police escorted Ingeborg Ydstie, director of the Munch Museum, to a parked van. "There were 20 to 30 policemen standing in a row; it was quite emotional," Ydstie said. "Then they opened the back of the van and there the paintings were. Tears filled my eyes."[8]

In addition to the recovery of the paintings, Ydstie had another reason for being emotional: Both works had sustained considerable damage. Numerous holes were punched in *Madonna*. *The Scream* had been wrapped in a damp blanket for months, and a huge stain covered much of the painting. Some of the original pigment had disappeared.

In spite of the damage, officials at the Munch Museum decided to display the two works in a special exhibition in 2008. "The works will be conserved before the exhibition, but some of the damages on *The Scream* will show," explained museum curator Petra Pettersen. "This does not interfere with the painting's unique artistic quality."[9]

Other Famous Art Thefts

Painted by Italian artist Leonardo da Vinci, the *Mona Lisa* is one of the world's most famous works of art. On August 22, 1911, newspapers around the world reported that the *Mona Lisa* had been stolen from the Louvre Museum in Paris. After more than two years with no leads or clues, an Italian named Vincenzo Perugia approached an art dealer in Florence, Italy, and said he had the painting. The dealer contacted police, and Perugia readily confessed to the crime. He had been an employee of the Louvre. He hid in a broom closet when his shift was over and waited for several hours, then cut the painting out of the frame, rolled it up, put it under his coat, and walked out. He said that the painting belonged in Italy, where it had been painted, rather than in France. Authorities disagreed and returned the painting to the Louvre.

Russborough House, one of the largest private estates in Ireland, features an art collection valued at tens of millions of dollars. Because it is situated on extensive grounds at least twenty minutes from the nearest police station, thieves have struck it four times: in 1974, 1986, 2001, and 2002.

The biggest theft in modern times was in 1990, at the Isabella Stewart Gardner Museum in Boston. Despite strict orders not to open the doors at night, two young guards—who were art students—admitted two men in police uniforms at 1:30 A.M. The men tied up the guards, spent nearly an hour and a half strolling leisurely through the galleries, then took thirteen paintings and drawings valued at $300 million.

Portrait of Jacob de Gheyn III, Rembrandt

"Tell them they'll be hearing from us,"[10] one of the men said as he left. No one ever has heard from the thieves, and the case remains unsolved.

The most frequently stolen painting is Rembrandt's *Portrait of Jacob de Gheyn III*, which has been taken four times since 1966 and returned anonymously each time. As a result, it is nicknamed the Takeaway Rembrandt. Its small size—about eleven inches by nine and a half inches—is probably a factor in its frequent disappearances.

The Dead Mother shows Munch's feelings at the death of his mother when he was just five years old. She died more than 30 years before Munch painted the work in 1899, but he still had vivid memories. Here, the child turns her back on her mother as if she is trying to deny what has just happened. As is the case with *The Scream*, the little girl holds her hands over her ears. The cry of pain she hears is very intense.

two

Of Birth and Death

The story of *The Scream* began almost a century and a half before its two high-profile thefts. At that time Norway wasn't an independent country. It had been under Swedish control for nearly five decades.

"On the 12th of December my eldest son was born to the world, and was christened Edvard after my beloved father. May he die the righteous death, and his passing be as his."[1]

In this unusual way Christian Munch recorded the birth of his first son in the family Bible late in 1863. Most parents look forward to a long and happy life for their newborn, rather than focusing on the child's eventual death. Christian Munch's obsession with death would accompany Edvard his entire life. When he lay in his coffin eighty years later, a portrait he had painted of his father overlooked the scene.

"My father was temperamentally nervous and obsessively religious," Munch wrote. "From him I inherited the seeds of madness. The angels of fear, sorrow and death stood by my side since the day I was born. They followed me when I played—followed me everywhere. Followed me in the spring sun and in the glory of summer."[2]

Christian Munch was an army doctor who was well into his forties when he met Laura Bjølstad in a country town. She was just twenty-one at the time of their marriage in October 1861. The couple had a daughter, Sophie, in 1862, and Edvard followed a year later. He was a sickly boy and at first his very survival seemed in doubt. It is likely that his frail constitution owed something to his mother, whose own mother and sister had died of tuberculosis, a leading cause of death in the nineteenth century. In spite of her youth, Laura Munch was already suffering from ill health when Edvard was born.

The year after Edvard's birth, the family moved to Christiania (the spelling was later changed to Kristiania), Norway's capital. (In 1925 the city's name was changed back to Oslo, its historic name.)

Two more children followed—Peter in 1865 and Laura in 1867—and the rigors of childbirth probably worsened Laura's condition. It didn't help matters that she became pregnant yet again soon after baby Laura's birth. Early in 1868, she gave birth to Inger.

After Inger's arrival, Christian moved his family to a larger apartment. Their new kitchen window had a view of the surrounding landscape, and the dying Laura spent many hours there. This eventually became the subject of Edvard's painting *Dead Mother with Spring Landscape.*

A few months after the move, young Edvard took his final walk with his mother. The memory remained with him for the rest of his life, and he recorded it in his painting *Outside the Gate.*

Laura Munch died a few days after Christmas. The memory of her death was burned into Edvard's consciousness. Writing in the third person, he said, "She made them [Edvard and Sophie] promise her to hold fast to Jesus so that they would all meet again in heaven. They did not completely understand what she was saying—but they thought it was so terribly sad they both began to cry, to weep and weep."[3]

One day after their mother's death, Edvard and Sophie were arguing. Their father appeared in the doorway. " 'Mama sees you,' he said. Edvard looked up towards the door, expecting her to open it and stand there, tall in her black dress—and alive."[4] Christian Munch would often invoke the memory of his dead wife to induce guilt in the children and make them behave.

Laura's sister, Karen Bjølstad, moved in and took over the household. Christian, who was depressed by his wife's death, became especially strict and obsessively religious. It was often hard for Munch to get along with his father.

"When anxiety did not possess him, he would joke and play with us like a child," Munch wrote. "When he punished us . . . he could be insane in his violence. In my childhood I always felt that I was treated unjustly, without a mother, sick, and with the threat of punishment in Hell hanging over my head."[5]

His aunt's obvious affection helped him deal with his father's rages. She also encouraged him in his artistic talents, which became evident within a year or two after his mother's death. A procession of sightless people served as an early inspiration. "I remember at the age of seven lying down on the floor with a piece of coal and drawing the blind,"[6] he said.

He continued to pursue his artistic interests as he grew older. Ordinary household objects were some of his primary subjects. He was all too familiar with them because he was sick so often, and sometimes spent weeks or even months at home.

Munch wasn't the only sick one in the family. In 1877, at the age of fifteen, Sophie caught tuberculosis and died. It was a harsh blow for the thirteen-year-old Edvard, who had been especially close to his older

Sister Inger, painted in 1884, is one of Munch's early works. Inger was his youngest sister. Though she is wearing black in mourning, Inger's face shows her determination to keep on living. He exhibited the painting in one of his earliest exhibitions, at Antwerp, Belgium, in 1885.

sister. At about the same time that Sophie died, Edvard's younger sister Laura was starting to show signs of the insanity that would plague her for most of her life. As a result, he became familiar with death and inner anguish at an impressionable age. These two themes would dominate his work.

In the fall of 1879, Munch began attending the Kristiania Technical College with the intention of becoming an engineer. His father believed that technology was the wave of the future and wanted to make sure that his son would have a secure way of earning a living.

Edvard didn't stay there long. He often missed classes because of his ill health and fell behind in his studies. He did have energy to pursue his art. The following May, he bought oil paints and brushes and noted in his diary, "Today I am making an oil painting of Old Aker Church."[7] On November 1, he made a far more momentous entry: "I have in fact made up my mind to become a painter."[8]

He dropped out of the technical college and registered as a student at the Royal School of Design in Kristiania. Within a year, he left the school. Christian Krohg, a well-established Norwegian painter, offered free instruction to Munch and several other young painters. They rented a studio in the center of the city close to where Krohg lived.

Munch quickly began having success. In the spring of 1883, he had a painting in Kristiania's Industry and Art Exhibition; in December he showed some works in the Autumn Exhibition. Still more exhibitions would follow.

His accomplishments attracted the notice of one of the city's leading painters, Frits Thaulow. Thaulow used his position and prestige to help young artists, and he generously offered to send Munch to Paris for a few weeks. So Munch, at the age of twenty-one, went abroad for the first time in the spring of 1885. This trip to Paris gave Munch a decades-long love of travel and living abroad. It also brought into clearer focus the difference between the provincial atmosphere in Kristiania and the worldly sophistication of Paris, the center of the art world at that time.

He had already become influenced by a group of radical thinkers and artists in the Norwegian capital, led by a man named Hans Jaeger. Jaeger had encouraged him to keep a detailed journal of his thoughts and feelings. The group also emphasized the idea of personal freedom rather than following conventional ways of behavior.

Soon after returning home from Paris, Munch met Millie Thaulow, Frits Thaulow's married sister-in-law. He began a love affair with her. Because of the strong sense of sin and morality drummed into him by his father, Munch felt shame and guilt over the affair—which only served to increase the anguish of his personal life. Still, the affair went on for several years.

Up to this point, Munch's painting had been largely influenced by two different artistic movements, both of which had originated in France. One was naturalism, painting in the open air rather than in a studio; the other was impressionism.

He soon realized that neither method was adequate for what he was trying to convey in his paintings. In 1886, he found what he considered to be a better way and painted his first masterpiece, *The Sick Child* (see page 20).

"I began as an impressionist but it was limited and I had to find another way of expressing the emotional turmoil I experienced," he wrote. "*The Sick Child* was the first break from Impressionism—I was searching for its expression."[9] The "turmoil" Munch referred to was the intense sorrow he felt over the death of his sister Sophie nearly a decade earlier.

It wasn't an easy process. "Over the course of that year, I made several changes to her, I scraped her, I let her dissolve into the soft paint and attempted over and over again to recapture that first impression, the pale translucent complexion against the linen sheets, the quivering mouth, the shaky hands."[10]

Many art historians believe the movement that would later be called expressionism began with this work. While expressionism isn't as well defined as other types of art, in general it refers to the artist's depiction of feelings aroused by a person or an event.

"In *The Sick Child* I broke new ground," he wrote. "No painting ever caused such offence in Norway. On the opening day, when I entered the gallery there was a crowd of people in front of the picture,—they were laughing and shouting."[11] One noted painter even came up to him. " 'Humbug painter!' he yelled in my face."[12]

Other people were more supportive, and by the spring of 1889 he was able to put on the first one-man show in Kristiania. Its success earned him an official government scholarship to return to Paris and study life drawings there. This scholarship would change the course of his life and within a few years catapult him to international recognition.

The Sick Child is considered to be Munch's first masterpiece; he completed it in 1886. It was based on his grief over the death of his sister Sophie. He spent a considerable amount of time on it. On several occasions, he scraped off something that he had painted so that he could make changes. Many people were shocked by the painting and criticized it.

A Brief History of Norway

Norwegian Landscape

While people have lived in Norway for thousands of years, it became powerful in the ninth century CE with the emergence of the Vikings. These were farmers, traders, explorers, and, most famously, fierce warriors who sailed their longboats thousands of miles across open oceans. Some historians believe that they were the first Europeans to reach North America, almost 500 years before Christopher Columbus.

One of the early Norwegian kings was Olav II, who later became a saint of the Catholic Church (and gave his name to an award that Munch would win in 1933). By the middle of the thirteenth century, Norwegian power reached its peak. It controlled Iceland and Greenland as well. About a century later, the Black Death killed up to half the population. Norway became part of the Kalmar Union, which also included Denmark and Sweden. Sweden left the union early in the sixteenth century, and Denmark became the senior partner. Many Norwegians refer to the centuries that followed as the "400-year night."

One of the major kings during this period was King Christian IV of Denmark. When Oslo, the Norwegian capital, burned down in 1624, he rebuilt the city and gave it the name of Christiania.

Denmark was defeated in 1814 during the Napoleonic Wars and had to give Norway to Sweden. The Danes tried to maintain control, and under their encouragement the Norwegians drew up a constitution on May 17 of that year, a date that is still celebrated in Norway. Swedish intervention prevented Norway from becoming independent at that time, but the Swedes allowed Norway to maintain the parliament (the Storting) that was called for in the constitution. By the end of the century, Norwegian nationalism was heightened and a war with Sweden seemed on the horizon. The situation was resolved peacefully, and Norway became independent in 1905. Prince Carl of Denmark was named king of Norway and took the throne as Haakon VII.

Except for the years of German occupation during World War II, Norway has been independent since 1905. In 2008, with a population of just over four and a half million, it had one of the highest standards of living in the world.

Many artist paint several self-portraits, and Munch was no exception. His *Self-portrait with Cigarette* was painted in 1895. It shows Munch with an anxious expression on his face. He became a heavy smoker, and in this painting he uses the cigarette smoke to cover up part of his body, giving the painting an air of mystery.

CHAPTER 3
three

The Scream

Munch had barely settled himself in Paris when he received shattering news. His father had suddenly become ill and died. The death hit Munch hard, especially since he wasn't able to return to Norway and attend the funeral. In spite of his differences with his father, he felt genuine affection for the man.

He became increasingly depressed and spent considerable time wandering through the streets of Paris. Some of the things he saw made a deep impression. He later wrote about how he'd changed in what became known as the St. Cloud Manifesto (St. Cloud is a suburb of Paris). He wrote that he would paint people "in that moment when they are no longer themselves but only one of thousands of links tying one generation to another generation. People should understand the sanctity of this and take off their hats as if they were in church. I would make a number of such paintings. No longer would interiors, people who only read and knit, be painted. There should rather be living people breathing and feeling, suffering and loving. I feel I have to do this. It would be so simple. The flesh would take on form and the colors come to life."[1]

Munch went back to Norway to spend the summer, then returned to France in the autumn when his scholarship was renewed. It was especially cold in Paris, so he spent several months in Nice (pronounced NEES) on the Mediterranean coast. In the summer of 1891, he again went back to Norway. As art historian Thomas M. Messer notes, "It is likely that had Munch died in 1891, he would have been mourned as Norway's white hope but would have remained unrecorded in the annals of an internationally oriented history of modern art."[2]

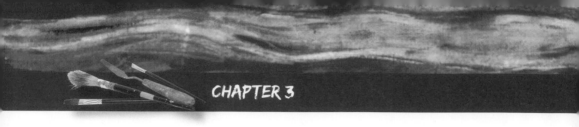

Because he had been ill so often and missed out on his studies, his scholarship was extended for a third year. Once again he spent most of his time in Nice. There, he would put the St. Cloud Manifesto into practice.

The new approach becomes apparent when two paintings on virtually the same subject are compared. Both are set on Karl Johan Street, the main thoroughfare in Kristiania. *Spring Day on Karl Johan Street,* painted in 1891, is bright. One can almost sense the exuberance of a warm day after the cold of the long Norwegian winter. The following year he painted *Evening on Karl Johan Street.* The crowd is no longer on the sidelines, but heading with haunted expressions toward the viewer. A lone figure walks in the opposite direction. This figure expresses the artist's sense of isolation and not being understood.

Evening on Karl Johan Street was among the first of a series of paintings Munch called the *Frieze of Life.* A frieze is a continuous band of artwork. Munch envisioned the paintings that composed the *Frieze* being exhibited next to each other, so that the viewer's emotional response to each painting would carry over to the next one.

Many art historians believe that *Evening on Karl Johan Street,* painted in 1892, reflects an upsetting personal experience. Munch had just run into the woman he loved on the street. She ignored him and continued on her way.

Meanwhile, many Norwegians believed that Munch didn't deserve the state scholarship for a third year. He was eager to show that it had been justified, so he opened a one-man show in September 1892 in Kristiania. Adelsteen Normann, a Norwegian painter who lived in Berlin, saw the exhibit. He was so impressed that he obtained an invitation to show Munch's works at the Artists' Union in Berlin.

The show opened in November and caused a sensation. Most German art at that time was realistic and emphasized sentimentality and patriotism. Many people called Munch's works an "insult to art," and the show had to close after a week. Munch was delighted. He realized that the uproar could attract people to exhibitions elsewhere: "I have never had such an enjoyable time—incredible that something as innocent as painting can cause such a stir,"[3] he wrote to his aunt.

The following year he painted *The Scream*. While he had been in Nice early in 1892, he wrote about his memory of an earlier event in Norway: "I was walking along the road with two friends. The sun began to set. I felt a twinge of melancholy. Suddenly the sky became bloody red. I stopped, leaned against the railing, dead tired, and I looked at the flaming clouds that hung like blood and a sword over the blue-black fjord and the city. My friends walked on. I stood there, trembling with fright. And I felt a loud, unending scream piercing nature."[4]

His friend Christian Skredsvig "later remembered that when he had been in Nice, Munch had often spoken of his desire to paint the *memory* of a sunset of 'coagulated blood.' Skredsvig reports that Munch 'talked himself sick about that sunset and how it had filled him with great anxiety.' "[5]

It's not certain when Munch witnessed this unsettling sunset. A team of astronomers maintain that it was linked to the eruption of the volcano Krakatau (sometimes spelled *Krakatoa*) in modern-day Indonesia in 1883. The eruption released tremendous amounts of ash into the air, which produced extraordinary and well-documented sunsets for several months.

The astronomers traveled to Oslo to check out their theory. One of them, Donald Olson, was also an art expert. He said, "We rounded a bend in the road and realised we were standing in the exact spot where Munch

Death in the Sickroom, dated in 1895, depicts the death of his sister Sophie. Unlike in *The Sick Child*, Munch barely hints at Sophie's presence. All the mourners are alone in their grief.

had been. We could see that Munch was looking to the south-west—exactly where the Krakatoa twilights appeared in the winter of 1883–84."[6]

Olson further noted that many of Munch's works were painted years after the actual events that inspired them. "The death paintings are particularly clear," he observed. "*Death of the Mother* and *Death in the Sickroom*, done in the 1890s, are based on the death of his mother in 1868 and the death of his sister in 1877. These experiences haunted him the rest of his life, as did the lurid, blood red sky."[7]

For Munch, "the rest of his life" lasted longer than five decades. While nothing else he painted would have the same impact as *The Scream*, it was just one part of the most astonishing bursts of creativity in art history.

The Eruption of Krakatau

On May 10, 1883, volcanoes on the small island of Krakatau began spewing dust and ash. Krakatau, located between the islands of Sumatra and Java in modern-day Indonesia, had been quiet for more than 200 years.

For several months, the ash clouds continued, often accompanied by small explosions. Inhabitants of Sumatra and Java became accustomed to the spectacle, and an almost festive atmosphere prevailed.

That mood changed abruptly on August 26, when a series of much larger eruptions began. They were just a warm-up for what happened the next morning. A massive eruption ripped the island apart, sending millions of tons of ash and dirt high overhead. The island became about a third of its former size as the sea rushed in.

The eruption generated a series of massive tsunamis that plunged ashore on nearby coastlines. At least 36,000 people perished. One survivor vividly recalled the panic: "There was a general rush to climb up in one particular place. This caused a great block, and many of them got wedged together and could not move. Then they struggled and fought, screaming and crying out all the time. Those below tried to make those above them move on again by biting their heels. A great struggle took place for a few moments, but . . . one after another, they were washed down and carried far away by the rushing waters. You can see the marks on the hillside where the fight for life took place. Some dragged others down with them. They would not let go their hold, nor could those above them release themselves from this death-grip."[8]

The sound of the explosion could be heard as far away as Australia. The debris in the atmosphere slowly ranged around the world, darkening skies for months and creating patterns such as the blood-red sunsets that likely were the inspiration for *The Scream.*

Aerial view of Krakatau

About forty-five years later, a small island called Anak Krakatau ("Child of Krakatau") emerged in the center of the area where the land had disappeared. The new island has minor volcanic eruptions almost every year, though they do not present much danger.

Munch painted *Anxiety* shortly after *The Scream*. The painting is set in virtually the same place as *The Scream*, and the expressions are almost the same as in *Evening on Karl Johan Street*. Even though the people appear well-dressed and prosperous, they don't seem very happy. It is almost as if they are attending a funeral.

four

The *Frieze* and Gunfire

Munch created many significant works in a period of just two or three years as he continued to develop the *Frieze*. As Alf Bøe of the Munch Museum points out, "[The *Frieze*] deals with the grand themes of love, anxiety, and death—major and harrowing forces in the course of man's life."[1]

In the catalog for a 1918 exhibition of the *Frieze* in Kristiania, Munch explained, "I painted picture after picture based on these visual impressions according to my emotional state at the time. . . . Like a phonograph [sic], I wanted to reproduce my moods by painting the colours, lines and shapes that I had seen in a particular state of mind."[2]

The "moods" Munch reproduced in the *Frieze* include the following:

- *Death in the Sickroom* (page 26) deals with the same subject as *The Sick Child* (page 20), but the emphasis is different. Munch shows only the back of the dying child and places her in the background, while the six mourners either face the artist or are seen in profile. They are all isolated from one another, incapable of offering any consolation.

- In *The Kiss*, the faces of the two lovers merge into a single mass of flesh. Munch feared that people in love would lose their individuality.

- *The Vampire* (page 11) shows a woman looming over a man, apparently sinking her teeth into the back of his neck. In an 1893 article about Munch's art, Polish poet Stanislaw Przybyszewski (who gave the work its current name; Munch's original title was *Love and Pain*) explained that the man in the painting "cannot free himself from the vampire, nor can he free himself of the pain, and the woman will always be sitting there, forever biting with a thousand vipers' tongues, with a thousand poison fangs."[3]

• Many people associate the color green with jealousy, and Munch's *Jealousy* is predominantly green. A man in the foreground scowls, while a woman in the background (perhaps the subject's wife) talks with another man.

• *Madonna* (page 31), stolen with *The Scream* in 2004, conveys two almost opposite ideas. One is the traditional association of the term *Madonna* with Mary, the mother of Jesus. The female figure has a small red halo behind her head. But she also seems to express feelings of love and the anguish that love can cause. "Your face embodies all the beauty of the world," Munch wrote. "Your lips, as crimson as a ripe fruit, are half open as if to express pain."[4]

In the fall of 1895, Munch had another exhibition in Kristiania. Famed Norwegian playwright Henrik Ibsen saw it. According to Munch, his painting *Woman in Three Stages* became the inspiration for Ibsen's play *When We Dead Awaken*. Published in 1899, it was Ibsen's final stage work.

Early the following year, Munch returned to Paris, hoping to make his mark there. He exhibited at the Salon des Indépendants. He also made a number of lithographs and woodcuts from the *Frieze of Life,* and illustrated programs for Ibsen's plays.

Meanwhile, his works were becoming more respected back home, so he held still another exhibition in Kristiania in the fall of 1897.

At about this time, Munch met Mathilde "Tulla" Larsen, the daughter of a prosperous wine seller in Kristiania. Early the following year they traveled to Italy, where Munch wanted to study Renaissance art. Soon, he knew the relationship was over. Edvard was reluctant to marry because of his family's history of illness. "Should we sick people establish a new home with the poison of consumption [tuberculosis] eating into the tree of life—a new home with doomed children—,"[5] he wrote.

The title *Madonna* is usually associated with Mary, the mother of Jesus. In *Madonna*, which Munch painted in 1894–1895, the halo is a part of this association. Yet everything else in the work is very different from traditional depictions of Mary.

Ashes, painted in 1894, shows the end of a love affair. The man in the foreground appears to be grieving at his loss. The forest in the background is dark and forbidding.

He underestimated the strength of Tulla's passion. She was thirty years old, beyond the customary age of marriage at that time, and may have seen the artist as her last hope. Even though they didn't spend much time together, in Tulla's mind the relationship still existed, and she continued to pursue him. Munch put most of his energy into avoiding her. His increasing anxiety made it virtually impossible for him to work.

The situation came to a head in 1902. A mutual acquaintance told Munch that Larsen would kill herself if he didn't meet with her. No one is sure about the exact sequence of events that followed. According to Munch, "Hardly had I entered the room when she sprang out of bed and said: 'You love me, Edvard. I knew you would come.' We quarreled and finally she produced a revolver and threatened to shoot herself. I did not believe her, but of course

The Dance of Life, painted in 1899–1900, illustrates several of Munch's most common themes. The young girl on the left seems optimistic as she looks at budding flowers. The woman in the center is about to engulf her male dance partner. And the woman on the right, an older version of the girl on the left, wears black and appears bitter.

I had to be chivalrous and put my hand over the revolver. And don't think [she] failed to press the trigger!"[6]

The bullet shattered the middle finger of his left hand. Munch was afraid he'd bleed to death. He rushed to a doctor, who immediately operated on him. Munch refused anesthesia.

"I felt the knife cut its way through the flesh, it scraped against the bones and blood gushed forth," he wrote. "The operation lasted a long time. I saw my fingers and hand bloody and swollen like a glove. The pain caused sweat to form on my brow. . . . The flesh was cut, trimmed, pierced, sewn and the hand resembled a piece of chopped meat."[7] The disfigurement haunted him for the rest of his life, a constant reminder of what he considered the waste of more than three years.

Artistically, however, things were going well for Munch. *The Frieze of Life* was exhibited in Germany that same year and was received much more favorably than his earlier exhibition. A German art dealer agreed to sell his works. In addition, an eye doctor named Max Linde became his patron.

More successes followed. He showed in 1903 and 1904 in Paris, and did even better at an exhibition in Prague in 1905. Yet he still bore the effects of the Tulla Larsen affair. A combination of frayed nerves and excessive drinking and smoking kept him on edge. He spent most of the next several years out of Norway.

He had such a hard time forgetting the traumatic event that he used a famous event in French history, the murder of Jean-Paul Marat by Charlotte Corday, to depict what had happened. In 1906's *The Murderess*, he shows himself as Marat lying dead on a bed with bloody sheets, with Larsen depicted as a depressed Corday.

Also in 1906, Munch received a prestigious commission: to design the sets for a production of Ibsen's *Ghosts* in Berlin. Yet his mental condition continued to worsen. He returned to the Marat theme in 1907 with *The Death of Marat*, which was even more graphic than the previous painting. Both figures are naked and the amount of blood is much greater.

Eventually Munch found himself on the verge of a nervous breakdown. He voluntarily entered a clinic in Copenhagen, Denmark, where he underwent a number of different treatments, including electroshock therapy. He also promised that he would never again touch alcohol.

Munch continued to paint while he was at the clinic, and during his time there he received considerable recognition in Norway. He was awarded the Royal Order of St. Olav to honor his artistic achievements. Early in 1909, his works were exhibited in Kristiania. Not only was the exhibition a success with the people who visited, but the National Gallery also purchased a number of his works for permanent display.

Henrik Ibsen

During Henrik Ibsen's time, plays were expected to have happy endings. The main character would face challenges and overcome them; bad behavior would be punished.

Ibsen changed all that. He is regarded as the "father of modern drama," drama that strips away illusions and shows things as they really are.

Ibsen was born in 1828 into a prosperous family, which soon encountered serious financial problems. They had to move to a small farmhouse, and most of their friends deserted them. Ibsen was bitter about these circumstances, which affected the way he looked at life. Reportedly only one photo of him shows him smiling.

When he was fifteen, he left home to work in a pharmacy and wrote plays in his spare time. One of his plays was staged in 1851. It didn't do well, so he spent seven years working as a theatrical director and producer. He married in 1858, but lived in poverty for six years because the plays he wrote weren't successful. He left Norway in 1864 in a self-imposed exile, living mostly in Italy and Germany.

In 1865, Ibsen wrote *Brand,* his first work to receive positive reviews. Two years later, his play *Peer Gynt* was also well received. Other plays that followed include *A Doll's House* (1879), *Ghosts* (1881), and *An Enemy of the People* (1882).

Perhaps his best known play is *Hedda Gabler,* which premiered in 1890. Hedda has a boring marriage (as did Ibsen), so to amuse herself, she encourages a drunken poet in behavior that results in his suicide. Judge Brack, a family friend, learns of Hedda's involvement and threatens to expose her if she doesn't agree to be with him. Hedda kills herself at the end of the play.

Ibsen returned to Norway in 1891 as a famous playwright. On his seventieth birthday in 1898, he was honored as the world's greatest living dramatist. He suffered a stroke two years later and died in 1906.

Portrait of Henrik Ibsen, Munch

Munch appears to be bravely facing the end of his life in *Self-portrait Between the Clock and the Bed*, his final masterpiece. Dating between 1940 and 1942, the painting shows Munch as a frail old man. The clock without any numbers shows he is out of time, and for Munch a bed has often been a symbol of illness and death.

five

Success and Recognition

Munch emerged from the clinic in the spring of 1909 and returned to Norway, where he learned about an upcoming project. A new hall called the Aula was being built at Kristiania's university to celebrate its 100th anniversary. The structure's interior would be decorated with a series of murals, and more than twenty painters applied for the commission.

Munch won the competition, and his mural marked a change in his approach. "*The Frieze of Life* is the joys and sorrows of individual men closely analyzed," he wrote. "The University Decorations are the great, eternal powers of life."[1]

The mural consisted of three parts. One was *The Sun,* located on an end wall and casting its life-giving rays on both *History,* which represents Norway's past, and *Alma Mater,* which depicts its future. The contrast with the *Frieze* is obvious. In *The Scream,* for example, the sun is setting and creating a sense of extreme anxiety. In *The Sun,* the sun is rising, evoking optimism.

In preparation for his work on the mural, Munch rented a large house in the village of Kragerø and built an open-air studio. The surroundings there greatly inspired him. He even used his handyman, Børre Eriksen, as the model for the primary figure in *History.*

In 1912, Munch was invited to participate in an exhibition in Cologne, Germany, that showcased the most important figures in modern art. Thirty-two of Munch's paintings hung in the largest room in the exhibition. Other major figures included Vincent van Gogh, Paul Gauguin, and Paul Cézanne. "Here are gathered the Wildest things painted in Europe—I am a pure classicist and faded,"[2] he wrote to his friend Jappe Nilssen.

The following year he received another honor: his own room at the Autumn Exhibition in Berlin. He and up-and-coming Spanish painter Pablo Picasso were the only non-Germans to be invited. Edvard Munch was now clearly regarded as the equal of the greatest painters of the era.

In 1916, he bought a large estate in the country west of Kristiania. The property, which Munch called Ekely, included a spacious house as well as horses, cows, pigs, and dogs. It would be his home for the rest of his life.

He said, "The only real danger for me is to be unable to work."[3] To make sure that didn't happen, he built multiple outdoor studios and an indoor one where he could work during the often harsh Norwegian winters.

As art historian John Boulton Smith observed, "Munch increasingly came to regard his paintings as a family, which he needed to have around him. He now hardly ever sold paintings, and he made new versions of ones he no longer possessed, especially if he regarded them as belonging to a series."[4]

Not all his efforts were successful. He did not win a competition to decorate the stock exchange in Bergen, Norway. A sweeter deal came in 1922, when he was commissioned by the Freia Chocolate Factory in Oslo.

The "fishing life of a small coastal town,"[5] as Munch described it, with boats bobbing gently on the water and healthy young Norwegian women happily watering flowers and picking apples, couldn't have been farther from the haunting images of *The Scream* and much of his earlier work. A Norwegian newspaper that had often criticized him commented, "The large canteen at Freia's chocolate factory which was already a fine example of a friendly and beautiful place, has been given a new shine."[6]

By this time Munch had achieved substantial recognition, both in Norway and in other countries. His friend Jappe Nilssen said that exhibitions of his work throughout Europe were a "triumphal procession without equal."[7]

The artist suffered a health setback in 1930 when a blood vessel burst in one of his eyes, almost blinding him for a year. He recovered, and two years later German leader Paul von Hindenburg presented him with the Goethe Medal for Science and Art. Munch was particularly proud of this award; the only other Norwegian recipients had been Roald Amundsen, the first man to reach the South Pole, and sculptor Gustav Vigeland. In 1933, honoring his seventieth birthday, Munch received the Grand Cross of St. Olav.

Munch was well into his fifties when he painted *Nude by the Wicker Chair* in 1929. The swirl of colors illustrates his inner turmoil around women, and the large amount of space covered by the woman in the painting shows that he still regards women as being very powerful.

That same year, Hindenburg appointed Adolf Hitler as German chancellor. Joseph Goebbels, who would later become notorious for his writings and speeches on behalf of Hitler, wrote to Munch, "I greet you as the Greatest Painter of the Germanic World."[8] Addressing Munch in the third person, he continued, "His paintings, landscapes as well as representations of human beings are suffused by deep passion. . . . A powerful, independent strong-willed spirit—heir of Nordic culture—he frees himself of all naturalism and reaches back to the eternal foundations of National art-creating."[9]

Under the influence of Hitler's Nazi Party, which used violence and coercion to try to create a morally, racially, and culturally superior nation, the artistic landscape in Germany soon changed—and not in Munch's favor. In 1937, eighty-two of his paintings in Berlin were branded as "degenerate" and taken down as part of a larger crackdown. Grinning Germans gleefully made bonfires of thousands of works of art; most of Munch's works were saved.

Three years later, Hitler's armies invaded Norway. Munch was very upset and refused to have any contact with German officials or with the Norwegians who assisted them. The Norwegian puppet government, led by Vidkun Quisling, established an Honorary Board of Norwegian Artists and invited Munch to become a part of it. He emphatically refused. Because of his stature in the country, there was no point in having the board without him.

The refusal took a lot of courage, since the Nazis often dealt harshly with people who defied them. From that point on, Munch lived with the constant fear that he could be arrested and his "children"—his paintings—taken away.

In spite of his uneasiness, he continued to work. Perhaps his final masterpiece was *Self-portrait Between the Clock and the Bed*, painted between 1940 and 1942. It reveals a frank awareness of his impending demise. He stands, almost at rigid attention, between two symbols of death: a clock with no hands and a bed. The wall in a room behind him has hints of many of his paintings. A door opens into a narrow passage, its darkness reflecting death's uncertain journey.

Late in 1943, Edvard Munch contracted a severe case of pneumonia. He died at his beloved Ekely on January 23, 1944.

Soon after his death, it was revealed that he had bequeathed his entire body of work to the city of Oslo. It consisted of more than 1,000 paintings, nearly 5,000 drawings, and about 18,000 prints, in addition to his correspondence and other artifacts. Two years later, the Oslo city council decided to build a museum devoted entirely to the artist. It opened in 1963 to honor the one hundredth anniversary of Munch's birth.

The museum has no shortage of visitors. Munch has proved to be one of the major artists of the late-nineteenth and twentieth centuries. One reason for his enduring popularity is his vivid expression of the anxiety that many people feel. The terrible anguish of the central figure in *The Scream* is immediately and painfully obvious. The other two figures in the painting seem clueless about the main character's anxiety, which reinforces the idea that many people believe they are alone in the world, that they have no real connection to anyone else. And that is very frightening indeed.

Gustav Vigeland

In 1921, Norwegian sculptor Gustav Vigeland approached the Kristiania city council with an unusual proposition. The city had just torn down the ramshackle studio in which he had worked for many years. If the council would agree to build him a new studio with living quarters and support him for the rest of his life, he would bequeath all his unsold work to the city. In addition, he would create a sculpture park that he confidently predicted would attract worldwide attention. The council agreed.

Vigeland had been born in 1869 in a small farming community. By the time he was fifteen, it was evident that he had a talent for sculpting. After his father's death, he went to Kristiania to try to build a career. At first, he had little success. "I lived everywhere and nowhere, in attics and cellars and finally I had no proper food,"[10] he said.

A year later, he produced his first work. He spent major parts of the succeeding years in other European countries, where he began developing his two main themes: death and the relationship between men and women. He soon acquired a glowing reputation among his country's art critics, but found he couldn't make a living just doing sculpture on his own. Most of his income for more than two decades came from commissions and making busts of well-known countrymen.

An angry baby, in the Vigeland Sculpture Park, by Gustav Vigeland

After his agreement with the city, he set to work. The sculpture park he created is the most prominent feature in Frogner Park, a popular gathering spot. The highlight is *The Monolith,* a granite column that rises nearly sixty feet into the air. It took three craftsmen, working under Vigeland's close supervision, fourteen years to complete the 121 human figures that comprise it. The figures embrace each other as they rise toward heaven and their hope of salvation.

After Vigeland's death in 1943, his studio became a museum. His ashes are buried in its tower. The sculptor proved to be prophetic: The Vigeland Sculpture Park is indeed famous around the world.

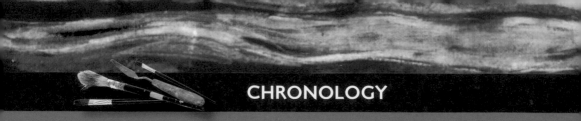

CHRONOLOGY

1863 Edvard Munch is born on December 12 in Löten, Norway.

1864 The Munch family moves to Christiania (Oslo), Norway.

1868 Edvard's mother, Laura, dies of tuberculosis.

1877 His sister Sophie dies of tuberculosis at the age of fifteen.

1879 Munch enters Kristiania Technical College.

1880 After deciding to become an artist, he leaves Kristiania Technical College and enrolls at the Royal School of Design.

1885 Munch travels to Paris, his first trip out of Norway.

1886 His painting *The Sick Child* causes a scandal at Kristiania's Autumn Exhibition.

1889 His father dies, which leads to a period of depression.

1892 An exhibition of Munch paintings in Berlin closes in a week due to protests.

1893 Munch paints *The Scream*.

1897 He meets Tulla Larsen.

1902 He is shot in the finger during an argument with Tulla.

1906 Munch provides set decoration for Berlin production of Henrik Ibsen's *Ghosts*.

1908 He has a nervous breakdown and is admitted to Dr. Daniel Jacobson's clinic in Copenhagen; is awarded the Royal Order of St. Olav.

1909 Munch returns to Norway.

1911 He wins competition to design murals at the Aula.

1912 Munch exhibits his work in Cologne, Germany, with Vincent van Gogh, Paul Gauguin, and Paul Cézanne.

1916 He buys an estate near Kristiania that he calls Ekely.

1922 He decorates workers' canteen at Freia Chocolate Factory.

1930 A blood vessel bursts in his eye, damaging his vision for almost a year.

1933 Munch is awarded the Grand Cross of St. Olav.

1937 German officials confiscate eighty-two of Munch's paintings in public galleries because they are deemed "degenerate art."

1940 Munch refuses to associate with Nazis after German invasion of Norway.

1944 He dies of pneumonia on January 23 at Ekely; leaves all his works to the city of Oslo.

1963 Munch Museum opens in Oslo.

1994 *The Scream* is stolen from the National Gallery in Oslo.

2004 Another version of *The Scream* is stolen at gunpoint from the Munch Museum and suffers damage.

2008 *The Scream* is exhibited in the Munch Museum, even though the damage from 2004 has not been completely repaired.

1814	Denmark is forced to yield control of Norway to Sweden.
1828	Norwegian playwright Henrik Ibsen is born.
1839	French painter Paul Cézanne is born.
1840	French impressionist painter Claude Monet is born.
1848	French painter Paul Gauguin is born.
1853	Dutch painter Vincent van Gogh is born.
1869	Norwegian sculptor Gustav Vigeland is born.
1874	French impressionist painters hold their first exhibition in Paris.
1879	The National Gallery opens in Kristiania.
1881	Spanish painter Pablo Picasso is born.
1883	Krakatau volcano erupts in Indonesia.
1886	Final impressionist exhibition takes place in Paris.
1890	Vincent van Gogh dies of a self-inflicted gunshot wound.
1903	Paul Gauguin dies.
1905	Norway gains its independence from Sweden.
1906	Henrik Ibsen dies; Paul Cézanne dies.
1910	Czech art historian Antonín Matejcek becomes first person to use the term *expressionism* to describe a certain form of art.
1911	The *Mona Lisa* is stolen from the Louvre Museum in Paris; it is recovered two years later.
1914	As World War I breaks out, Norway chooses not to take sides in the conflict.
1925	City of Kristiania changes its name to Oslo.
1933	Dictator Adolf Hitler is sworn in as chancellor of Germany on January 30.
1937	Germans destroy thousands of paintings that they consider to be degenerate; the toll includes some of Munch's works. Picasso paints *Guernica,* his most famous work, to protest the bombing of civilians during the Spanish Civil War.
1940	German troops invade Norway and take over the country.
1943	Gustav Vigeland dies.
1973	Pablo Picasso dies.
1996	Norway is ranked as third-largest exporter of crude oil in the world.
2007	GRIEG 2007 marks the 100th anniversary of the death of famed Norwegian composer Edvard Grieg.

SELECTED WORKS

CHAPTER NOTES

Chapter 1   Stolen—and Stolen Again!

1. Edward Dolnick, *The Rescue Artist: A True Story of Art, Thieves, and the Hunt for a Missing Masterpiece* (New York: HarperCollins, 2005), p. 8.

2. Ibid., p. 15.

3. Ibid., p. 8.

4. Ibid., p. 48.

5. Ibid., pp. 223–224.

6. Ibid., p. 160.

7. Ibid., p. 162.

8. Jonathan Jones, "The Bigger Picture," http://arts.guardian.co.uk/art/visualart/story/0,,2014954,00.html

9. Petra Pettersen, personal e-mail communication with the author, September 13, 2007.

10. Rachael Bell, "The Theft of the Mona Lisa," http://www.crimelibrary.com/gangsters_outlaws/outlaws/major_art_thefts/index.html

Chapter 2   Of Birth and Death

1. Sue Prideaux, *Edvard Munch: Behind the Scream* (New Haven, Connecticut: Yale University Press, 2005), p. 1.

2. Ibid., p. 2.

3. Ibid., p. 13.

4. Ibid., p. 14.

5. Edward Dolnick, *The Rescue Artist: A True Story of Art, Thieves, and the Hunt for a Missing Masterpiece* (New York: HarperCollins, 2005), p. 80.

6. Arne Eggum, *Edvard Munch: Paintings, Sketches and Studies,* translated by Ragnar Christophersen (New York: Clarkson Potter 1984), p. 16.

7. Ibid., p. 27.

8. Ibid.

9. Arne Eggum, "Edvard Munch: A Biographical Background," in *Edvard Munch: The Frieze of Life,* edited by Mara-Helen Wood (London: National Gallery Publications, 1993), p. 17.

10. Jose Maria Faerna, *Munch,* translated by Alberto Curotto (New York: Harry Abrams, 1996), p. 13.

11. Edvard Munch, "The Frieze of Life," in *Edvard Munch: The Frieze of Life,* edited by Mara-Helen Wood (London: National Gallery Publications, 1993), p. 13.

12. Ibid.

Chapter 3   The Scream

1. Reinhold Heller, *Munch: The Scream* (New York: Viking Press, 1973), p. 22.

2. Thomas M. Messer, *Edvard Munch* (New York: Harry Abrams, 1986), p 15.

3. Arne Eggum, *Edvard Munch: Paintings, Sketches and Studies,* translated by Ragnar Christophersen (New York: Clarkson Potter, 1984), p. 91.

4. Ashley Bassie, *Expressionism* (London: Sirrocco, 2005), p. 93.

5. Ibid.

6. Tim Radford, "Stratospheric Echo Locates Munch's *Scream*," http://arts.guardian.co.uk/news/story/0,,1103617,00.html

7. Ibid.

8. San Diego State University Department of Geological Sciences, *Krakatau, Indonesia* (1883), http://www.geology.sdsu.edu/how_volcanoes_work/Krakatau.html

Chapter 4   The *Frieze* and Gunfire

1. Alf Bøe, "Introduction," in *Edvard Munch: The Frieze of Life,* edited by Mara-Helen Wood (London: National Gallery Publications, 1993), p. 9.

2. Edvard Munch, "The Frieze of Life," in *Edvard Munch: The Frieze of Life,* edited by Mara-Helen Wood (London: National Gallery Publications, 1993), p. 13.

3. Ibid., p. 68.

4. Jose Maria Faerna, *Munch,* translated by Alberto Curotto (New York: Harry Abrams, 1996), p. 30.

5. Arne Eggum, *Edvard Munch: Paintings, Sketches and Studies,* translated by Ragnar Christophersen (New York: Clarkson Potter, 1984), p. 171.

6. *TIME* Magazine, "Expressionism's Father [obituary]," http://www.time.com/time/magazine/article/0,9171,791335,00.html?promoid=googlep

7. Sue Prideaux, *Edvard Munch: Behind the Scream* (New Haven, Connecticut: Yale University Press, 2005), p. 223.

Chapter 5   Success and Recognition

1. Reinhold Heller, *Munch: The Scream* (New York: Viking Press, 1973), p. 99.

2. Munch Museum, http://www.munch.museum.no/?id=&mid=&lang=en

3. John Boulton Smith, *Munch* (London: Phaidon Press, 1977), p. 23.

4. Ibid.

5. Sue Prideaux, *Edvard Munch: Behind the Scream* (New Haven, Connecticut: Yale University Press, 2005), p. 303.

6. Ibid.

7. Munch Museum. http://www.munch.museum.no/?id=&mid=&lang=en

8. Prideaux, p. 313.

9. Ibid.

10. Vigeland Museum and Park, *Gustav Vigeland* (1869–1943), http://www.museumsnett.no/vigelandmuseet/3vigeland/3a_biografi/engelsk/3aframeset.html

FURTHER READING

For Young Adults
Faerna, Jose Maria. *Munch.* Translated by Alberto Curotto. New York: Harry Abrams, 1996.
Holme, Merilyn, and Bridget McKenzie. *Expressionists.* Chicago: Heinemann, 2002.
Raimondo, Joyce. *Express Yourself!: Activities and Adventures in Expressionism.* New York: Watson-Guptill, 2005.

Works Consulted
Bassie, Ashley. *Expressionism.* London: Sirrocco, 2005.
Dolnick, Edward. *The Rescue Artist: A True Story of Art, Thieves, and the Hunt for a Missing Masterpiece.* New York: HarperCollins, 2005.
Eggum, Arne. *Edvard Munch: Paintings, Sketches and Studies.* Translated by Ragnar Christophersen. New York: Clarkson Potter, 1984.
Eggum, Arne, Reinhold Heller, Carla Lathe, and Gerd Woll. *Edvard Munch: The Frieze of Life.* Edited by Mara-Helen Wood. London: National Gallery Publications, 1993.
Faerna, Jose Maria. *Munch.* Translated by Alberto Curotto. New York: Harry Abrams, 1996.
Heller, Reinhold. *Munch: The Scream.* New York: Viking Press, 1973.
Messer, Thomas M. *Edvard Munch.* New York: Harry Abrams, 1986.
Pettersen, Petra (Curator of Munch Museum). Personal e-mail communication with author, September 13, 2007.
Prideaux, Sue. *Edvard Munch: Behind the Scream.* New Haven, Connecticut: Yale University Press, 2005.
Smith, John Boulton. *Munch.* London: Phaidon Press, 1977.

On the Internet
BBC News: "Queen Admires Most Stolen Painting"
 http://news.bbc.co.uk/1/hi/uk/764190.stm
Bell, Rachael. "The Theft of the Mona Lisa"
 http://www.crimelibrary.com/gangsters_outlaws/outlaws/major_art_thefts/index.html
Bloom, Harold. "Henrik Ibsen (1828–1906)"
 http://www.kirjasto.sci.fi/ibsen.htm
GoNorway: *Edvard Munch*
 http://www.gonorway.no/norway/sidevisning.php?id=35
GoNorway: *Gustav Vigeland*
 http://www.gonorway.no/go/vigeland.html
Jones, Jonathan. *Guardian Unlimited,* "The Bigger Picture"
 http://arts.guardian.co.uk/art/visualart/story/0,,2014954,00.html
Lambert, Tim. "A Brief History of Norway"
 http://www.localhistories.org/norway.html
Munch Museum
 http://www.munch.museum.no/?id=&mid=&lang=en
Munch Museum: "Munch and Ibsen"
 http://www.munch.museum.no/media/docs/26-06-2006-v6N2RhdD57rL4Pe.doc
Radford, Tim. *Guardian Unlimited,* "Stratospheric Echo Locates Munch's Scream"
 http://arts.guardian.co.uk/news/story/0,,1103612,00.html
San Diego State University Department of Geological Sciences: *Krakatau, Indonesia* (1883)
 http://www.geology.sdsu.edu/how_volcanoes_work/Krakatau.html
TIME Magazine: "Expressionism's Father [obituary]"
 http://www.time.com/time/magazine/article/0,9171,791335,00.html?promoid=googlep
Vigeland Museum and Park: *Gustav Vigeland* (1869–1943)
 http://www.museumsnett.no/vigelandmuseet/3vigeland/3a_biografi/engelsk/3aframeset.html

artifacts (AR-tuh-faks)—Human-made objects, usually from a particular time period.

bequeath (bee-KWEETH)—To leave personal items to someone else at the time of death.

canteen (kaan-TEEN)—Small cafeteria or break room.

chancellor (CHAAN-suh-lur)—Head of government in a European country.

coagulated (koh-AAG-yoo-lay-tud)—Thickened, clotted.

degenerate (dih-JEH-nuh-ret)—In a lower, corrupt condition.

electroshock therapy (ee-LEK-troh-shok THAYR-uh-pee)—Using electrical impulses through the brain as a medical treatment for mental health problems.

expressionism (ek-SPREH-shuh-ni-zum)—An art style that shows how the artist was feeling at a particular time.

felons (FEH-luns)—Criminals.

impressionism (im-PREH-shuh-nih-zim)—Type of painting that suggests an effect or impression of the subject, without including precise details.

lurid (LUR-id)—Shocking, gruesome, horrifying.

manifesto (maan-uh-FESS-toh)—Written statement detailing the views of its author.

patron (PAY-trun)—Person who financially supports an artist.

puppet government—Government appointed by an outside authority, which dictates its rules and procedures.

sublime (sub-LYM)—Elevated thought or expression.

turmoil (TUR-moyl)—Extreme confusion or commotion.

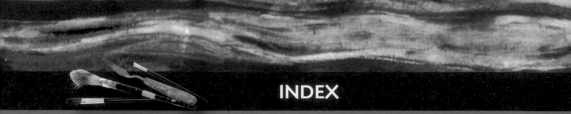

INDEX